P9-DTJ-121

HORSEPOWER

DEMOLITION DERBY CARS

by Mandy R. Marx

Reading Consultant:

Barbara J. Fox

Reading Specialist

North Carolina State University

Capstone *press*

Mankato, Minnesota

Blazers is published by Capstone Press,
151 Good Counsel Drive, P.O. Box 669, Mankato, Minnesota 56002.
www.capstonepress.com

Library of Congress Cataloging-in-Publication Data
Marx, Mandy R.
   Demolition derby cars/by Mandy R. Marx.
   p. cm.—(Blazers. Horsepower)
   Includes bibliographical references and index.
   ISBN-13: 978-0-7368-5472-6 (hardcover)
   ISBN-10: 0-7368-5472-X (hardcover)
   ISBN-13: 978-0-7368-6893-8 (softcover pbk.)
   ISBN-10: 0-7368-6893-3 (softcover pbk.)
   1. Automobiles—Juvenile literature. 2. Demolition derbies—
Juvenile literature. I. Title. II. Series.
TL147.M37 2006
629.222—dc22   2005020094

Summary: Discusses demolition derby cars, their main features,
   and how they compete.

Editorial Credits
Jenny Marks, editor; Jason Knudson, set designer; Thomas
   Emery, book designer; Jo Miller, photo researcher; Scott
   Thoms, photo editor

Photo Credits
Corbis/Duomo, 28–29
DENT/Craig Melvin, cover, 5, 6–7, 8, 9, 12, 14, 15 (both), 16–17, 19, 20,
   21, 25, 26–27
Getty Images Inc./The Image Bank/Chuck Fishman, 11; Time Life
   Pictures/Henry Groskinsky, 23
OneBlueShoe, 24

Capstone Press thanks Todd Dubé, President of Demolition Events
National Tour (DENT), for his assistance in the preparation of
this book.

The author dedicates this book to her nephew Carter, a future
demolition derby driver.

1 2 3 4 5 6 11 10 09 08 07 06

TABLE OF CONTENTS

A Smashing Good Time

In the outdoor arena, an excited crowd counts down. "Three, two, one." Crash! The demolition derby begins.

DENT
NATIONAL CHAMPIONSHIP
DEMOLITION TEAM

D·E·N·T
emolition Events National Tour
www.DENTUSA.com

5.

Brightly painted cars attack each
other on the track. Hoods crumple
and tires pop. One by one, cars break
down. They are out of the competition.

The winner appears out of a
cloud of smoke and steam. His car
is the only one still moving.

BLAZER FACT

Some demo cars need
help leaving the track.
Forklifts remove these
crushed cars.

GETTING DERBY-READY

Most derby drivers fix up cars built in the 1980s. Old police cars and taxicabs have especially strong frames.

Demo cars must be ready for action. Crews take out all glass and any unneeded parts. They modify the engine for extra power.

BLAZER FACT

Drivers install pipes in the hood to release exhaust. The pipes are called "headers" or "zoomies."

The final step is to blast the cars
with color. Crews paint bright designs
all over the cars. They also add numbers
and sponsor names.

Demo Derby Car Diagram

No glass

DENT 1

Roll bar

No mirror

Zoomies

Bright paint

SAFETY FEATURES

Injuries spoil the fun of a demo derby. A roll bar prevents the roof from caving in on a driver.

Fires break out at demo derbies. The last thing drivers want is a gas leak. They keep the gas tank in the back seat. The tank is safer there.

Gas tank

Drivers cut holes in the hoods of their cars. Fire fighters can put out fires without lifting the hood!

21

CRASH COURSE

Demolition derbies became popular in the United States in the 1950s. Crowds loved watching old cars smash into each other.

County fairs have held demo derbies for years. In 1997, Todd Dubé formed the Demolition Events National Tour (DENT) to promote the sport.

BLAZER FACT

Demo derbies are held for minivans, motorcycles, and even combines.

DENT sponsors the National Championship Demolition Derby Series. The winner receives a ring, a trophy, and $10,000.

D·E·N·T

www.DENT

.com

D·E·N·T

www.DENTUSA.com

D·E·

www.DENT

G-FORCE
RACING GEAR

sfi MANUFACTURER
CLOTHING
3.2A/T

BLAZER FACT

DENT gives a Mad Dog award to the driver who makes the hardest hits.

MANGLED METAL!

GLOSSARY

arena (uh-REE-nuh)—a large building used for sports or entertainment events

demolition (dem-uhl-ISH-uhn)—when something is destroyed

exhaust (eg-ZAWST)—the waste gases produced by the engine of a motor vehicle

frame (FRAYM)—the main body of a car

modify (MOD-uh-fye)—to change

roll bar (ROHL BAR)—a steel pipe that is welded to a derby car to keep the roof from caving in

sponsor (SPON-sur)—a company or organization that gives a driver equipment or money to compete

READ MORE

Huff, Richard M. *Demolition Derby*. Race Car Legends. Philadelphia: Chelsea House, 2000.

Savage, Jeff. *Demolition Derby*. Action Events. Berkeley Heights, N.J.: Enslow Publishers, 2000.

Savage, Jeff. *Demolition Derby Cars*. Wild Rides. Mankato, Minn.: Capstone Press, 2003.

INTERNET SITES

FactHound offers a safe, fun way to find Internet sites related to this book. All of the sites on FactHound have been researched by our staff.

Here's how:

1. Visit *www.facthound.com*
2. Type in this special code **073685472X** for age-appropriate sites. Or enter a search word related to this book for a more general search.
3. Click on the **Fetch It** button.

FactHound will fetch the best sites for you!

INDEX